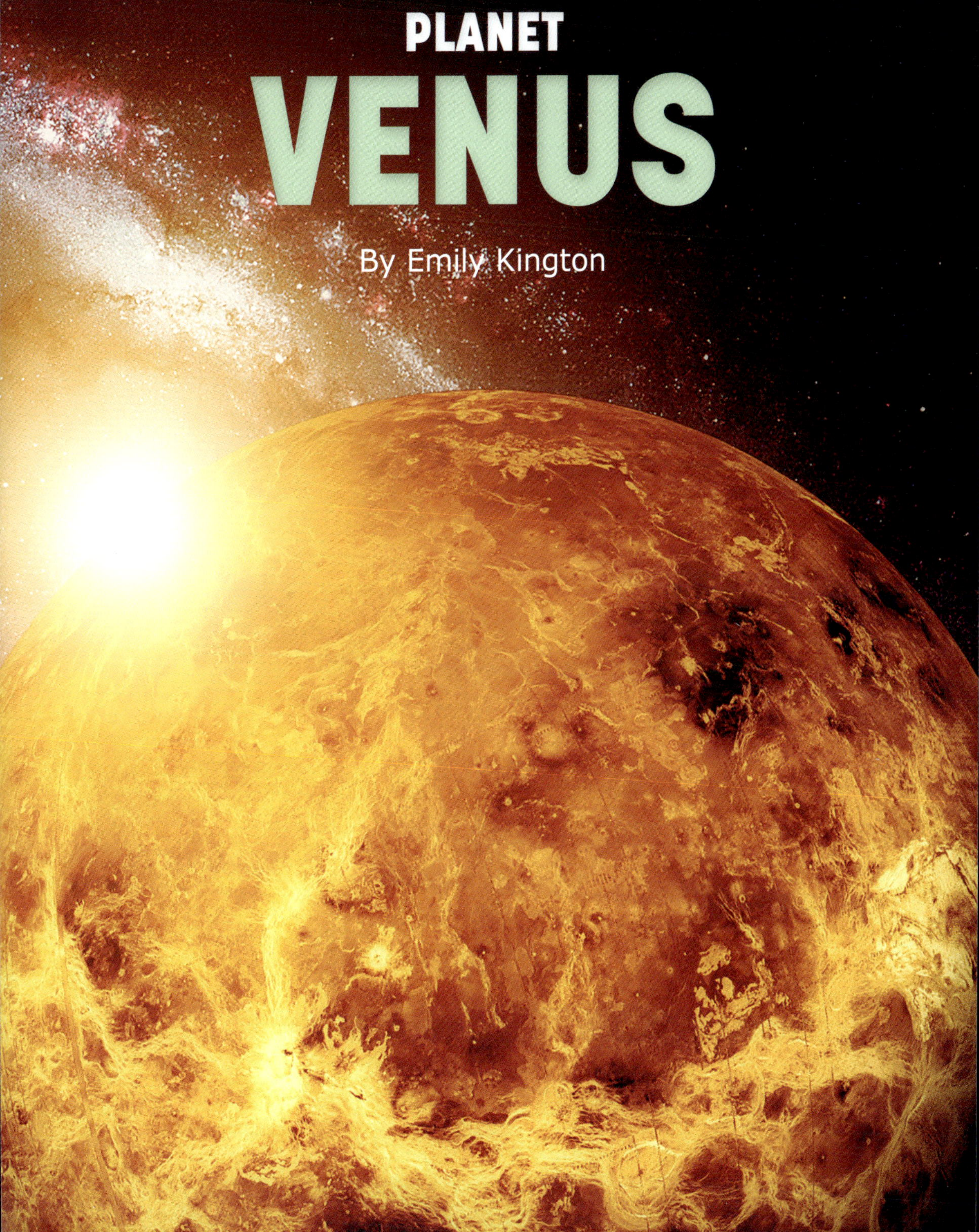
PLANET
VENUS
By Emily Kington

CONTENTS

First published in 2026 by Hungry Tomato Ltd
F15, Old Bakery Studios, Blewetts Wharf, Malpas Road, Truro, Cornwall, TR1 1QH, UK.

ISBN 9781835696767

Manufactured in the USA

Discover more at
www.hungrytomato.com

Front cover image is an edited image of Venus and the Veritas spacecraft.
Title page image is an edited image of Venus.
Contents page image is an edited image of Venus.

Words in **BOLD** can be found in the glossary.

WHERE IS VENUS?

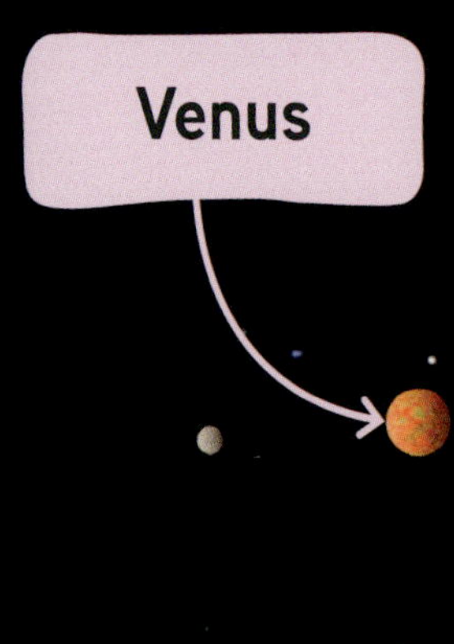

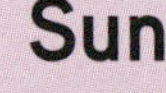

There are eight planets in our **solar system**. All of them travel around the Sun. Venus is the second closest planet to the Sun.

The time it takes a planet to travel around the Sun once is called a year. Venus travels around the Sun once every 225 **Earth days**. This journey is called Venus's **orbit**.

PLANET FACTS

Planets are always spinning. A day is the time it takes a planet to spin around once. Venus is the slowest-spinning planet – a day lasts the same as 243 Earth days!

Venus is one of two planets in our solar system that doesn't have a moon.

Whilst orbiting the Sun, Venus spins clockwise on its **axis**. This means that on Venus, the Sun rises in the west and sets in the east! The only other planet to do this is Uranus.

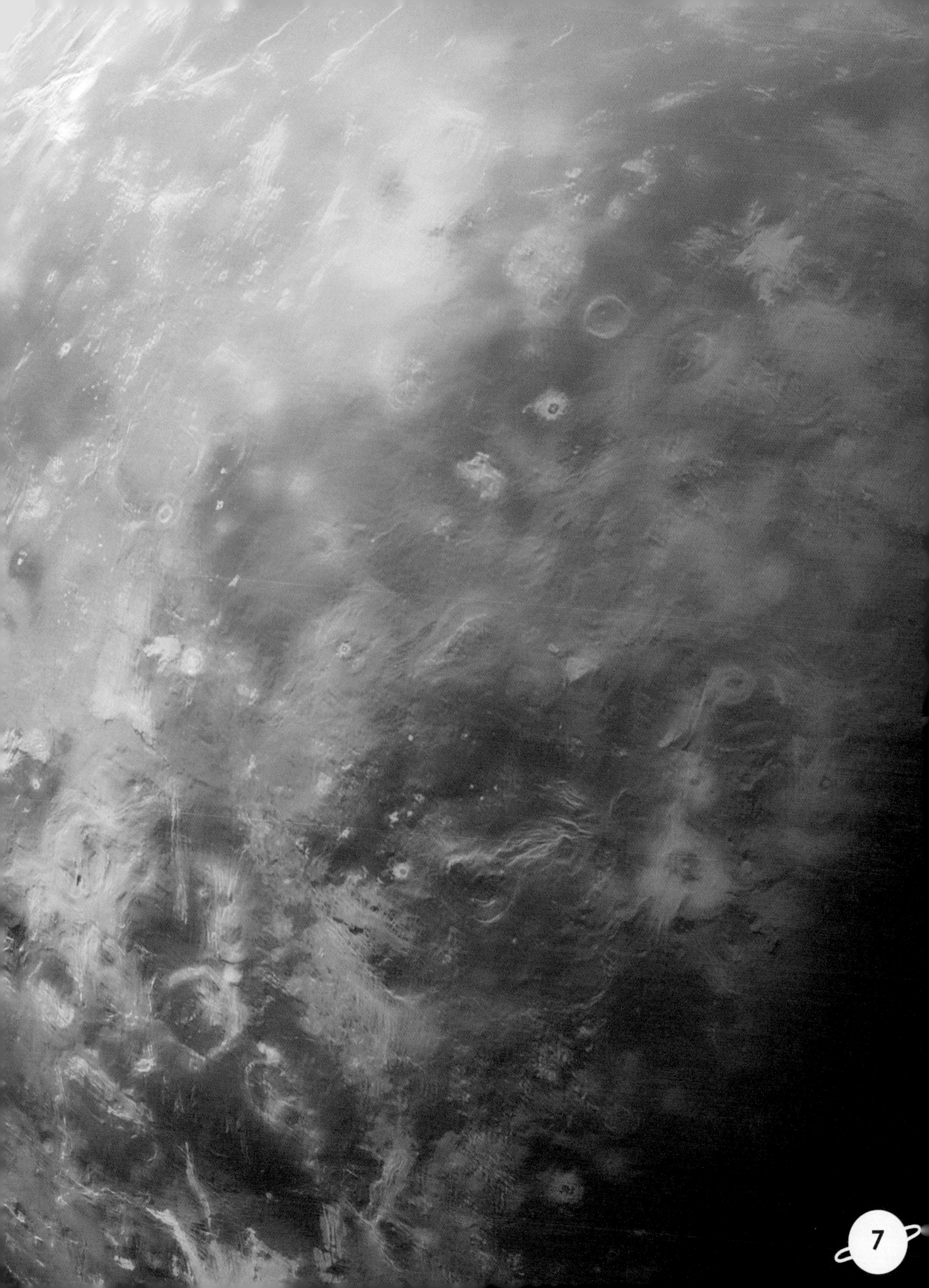

THE HOTTEST PLANET

Venus is covered in very thick layers of **atmosphere**, which traps in heat from the Sun like a blanket.

Even though it is not the closest planet to the Sun, Venus is the hottest planet in our solar system!

Its very thick clouds make it impossible to see its surface through a **telescope**!

The highest temperature on Mercury is about 806 °F (430 °C).

The top temperature on Venus is about 896 °F (480 °C)!

The highest temperature measured on Earth is 136 °F (58 °C).

CAN WE VISIT VENUS?

The thick atmosphere means Venus will never cool down enough for humans to ever visit.

There is a lot of pressure on its surface – Venus would crush humans immediately!

Space **probes** have taken pictures of the surface and spacecraft have landed, but not survived for much more than two hours.

Venera 12 is one of only a few spacecraft to have ever landed on Venus.

Venera 12

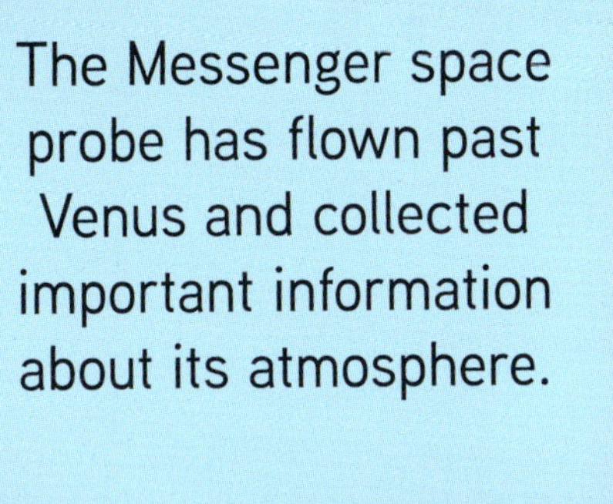

The Messenger space probe has flown past Venus and collected important information about its atmosphere.

NASA's Messenger space probe

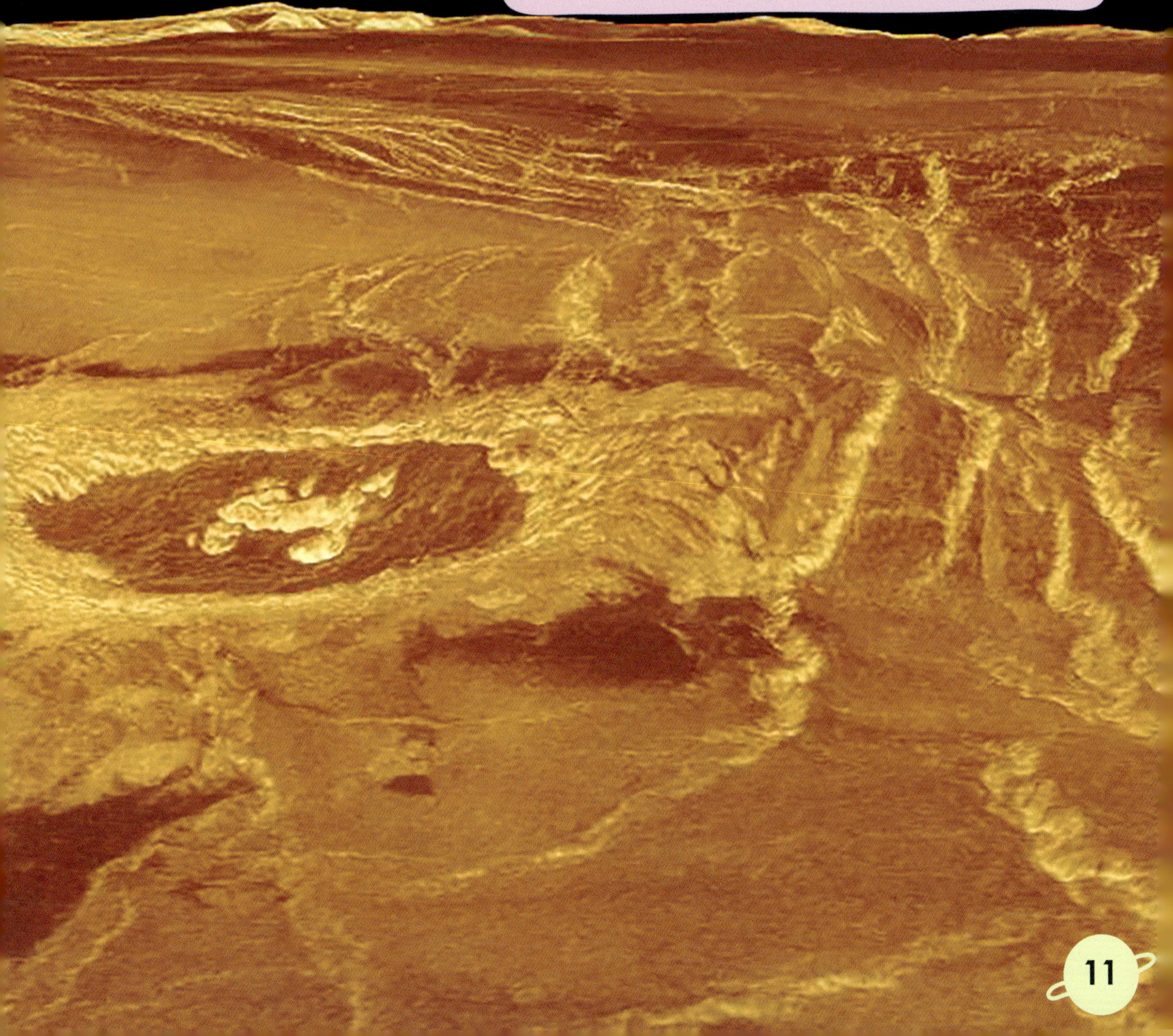

SPACE PROBE DISCOVERIES

Space probes and **landers** that have visited Venus are remotely controlled – scientists control them all the way from Earth!

These high-tech spacecraft have allowed us to discover what the surface of Venus looks like under its clouds.

Venus has valleys, **mountains** and thousands of volcanoes. The highest mountain, Skadi Mons, is almost 7 miles (11 kilometers) tall. That makes it taller than any mountain here on Earth.

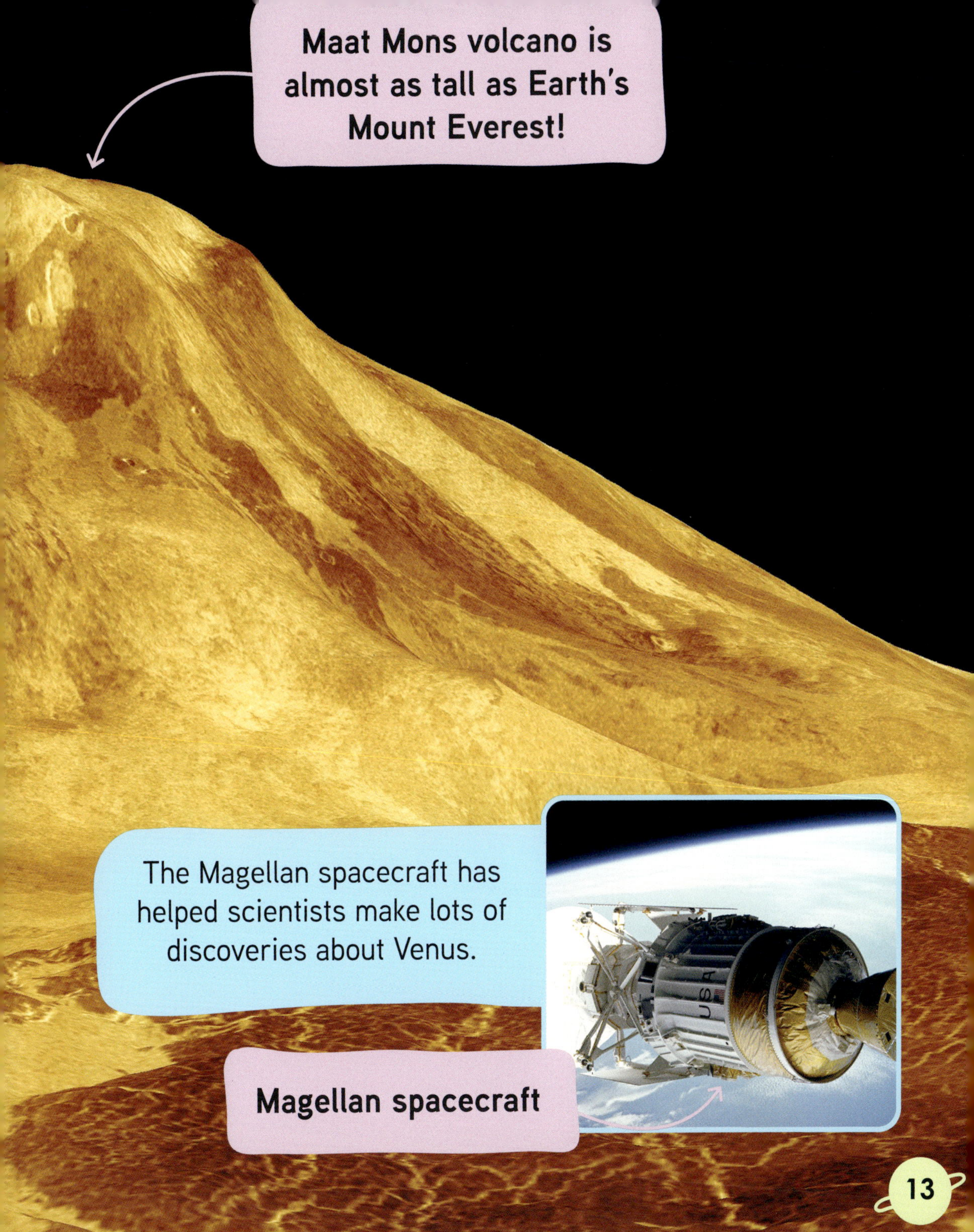
Maat Mons volcano is almost as tall as Earth's Mount Everest!
The Magellan spacecraft has helped scientists make lots of discoveries about Venus.
USA
Magellan spacecraft

FACT FILE

Venus is the brightest of all planets in our solar system.

Venus was named after the Roman goddess of love and beauty, because it was the most beautiful sight, shining in the morning and evening sky.

Venus shining bright

Because of this, people have always been curious about Venus, even before telescopes were invented.

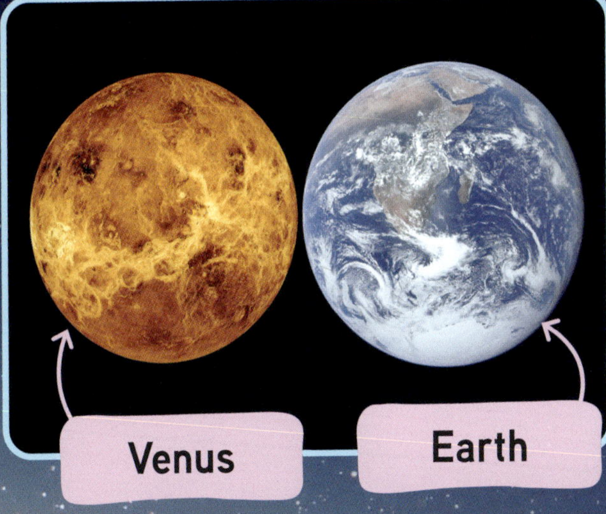

Venus is almost the same size as Earth. That's why it is often called Earth's twin! But the planet is deadly – there's no way humans could live there.

WHAT CAN WE SEE?

Venus is the third brightest natural object in the night sky after the Sun and Moon.

Clouds of **sulphuric acid** circle Venus and prevent us seeing its surface. The clouds **reflect** most of the sunlight that reaches it back into space...

Underneath Venus's clouds is a thick layer of carbon dioxide.

Venus

... making it look so bright and shiny it can sometimes be seen on a clear day!

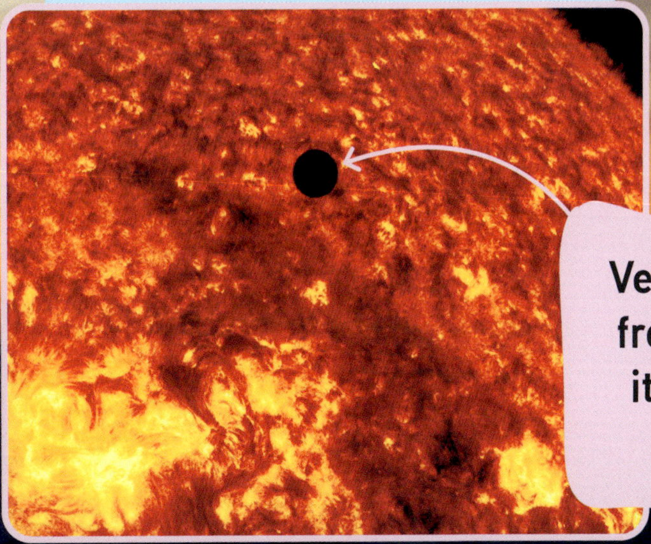

Venus may look bright from Earth, but when it passes the Sun, it looks black!

DISCOVERIES UNDER THE CLOUDS

In 1975, the Russian Venera 9 was the first lander to capture pictures of Venus's surface. After less than two hours, it was destroyed by the heat!

What it found was a rocky, **barren** surface and scorching temperatures, unable to support life.

In 1982, data and photographs collected from Venera 13 and 14 probes had scientists agreeing that liquid water does not exist on Venus. But maybe it could have once...

WHY DO WE STUDY VENUS?

Scientists that study other planets are like space detectives. Their work helps us understand more about our own planet.

Venus, like Earth, is actively changing. Knowing more about these changes can help us understand what is happening to our own climate.

Could Venus hold the secret to saving Earth?

Over 40 robotic missions have attempted to find out about Venus's past.

WHAT'S NEXT?

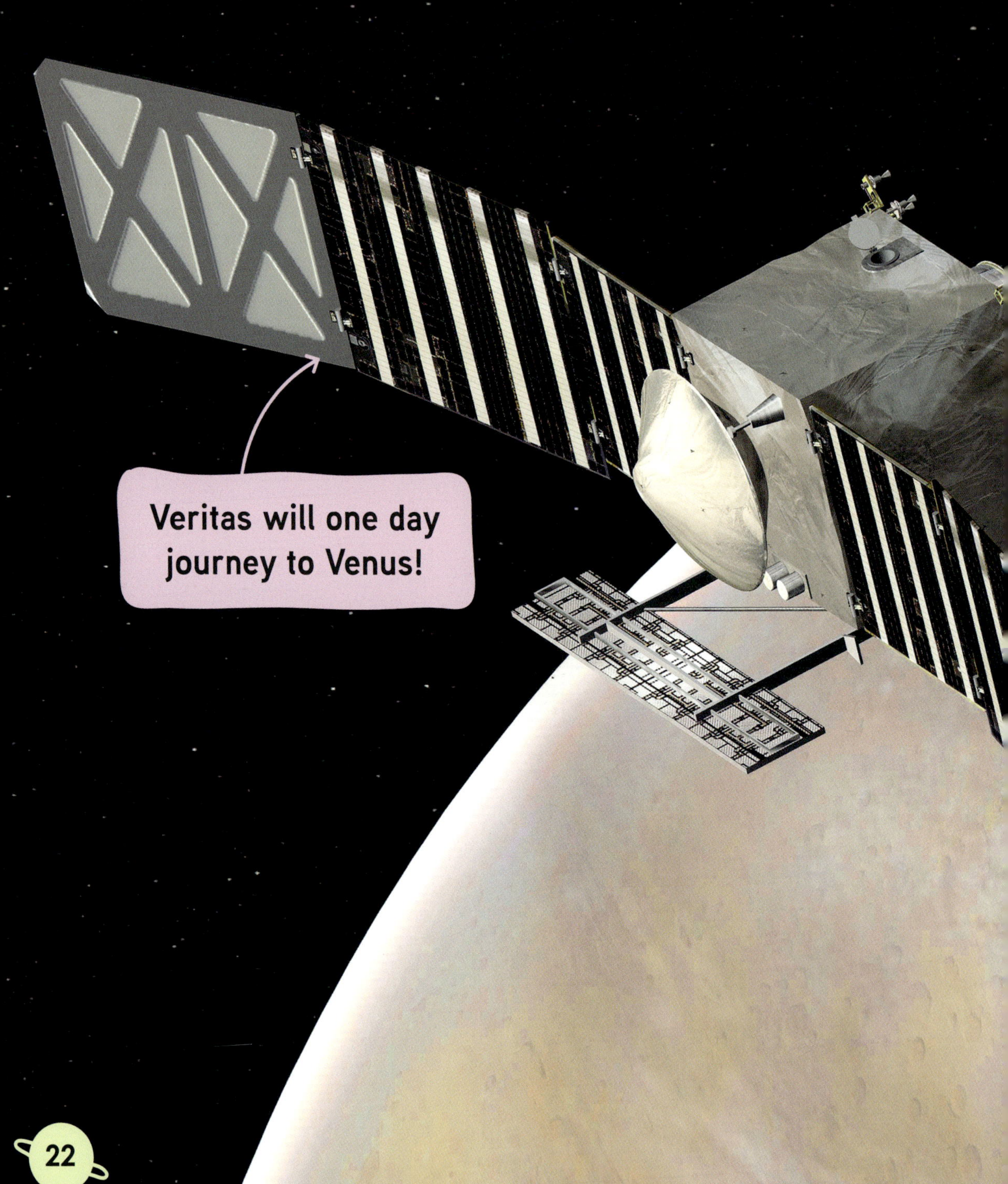

Missions to study space are planned by **space agencies** from all over the world. They build rockets and robots and sometimes send **astronauts** into space!

They will have to build tougher machines to withstand the heat and pressure on Venus, that can melt and break them in a very short time!

NASA and the **European Space Agency** are planning some exciting missions to learn more about why Venus is so different to Earth.

GLOSSARY

Astronauts – people trained to travel into outer space.

Atmosphere – the gases that surround a planet or star.

Axis – an invisible line that something spins around.

Barren – a place that is empty, where nothing grows.

Carbon dioxide – an invisible gas in the air.

Climate – long-term temperatures and weather conditions.

Earth days – the amount of time that a day lasts for on Earth (24 hours).

European Space Agency – a space agency run by a group of countries in Europe that studies outer space.

Landers – Spacecraft designed to land on the surface of other planets.

Mountains – rocky landforms that rise high above their surroundings.

NASA – the National Aeronautics and Space Administration is an agency that deals with space exploration.

Orbit – the path taken by one object circling around another object in space.

Pressure – a force that pushes on something.

Probes – uncrewed spacecraft sent to explore outer space.

Reflect – to shine back.

Solar system – the Sun and everything that moves around it.

Space agencies – organizations that design and launch missions to explore space.

Sulphuric acid – a very strong and dangerous liquid.

Telescope – an instrument that makes faraway objects appear bigger.

Picture credits:
(t=top; b=bottom; m=middle; l=left; r=right):

Wikipedia: By Don S. Montgomery, U.S. Navy (Ret.) - http://www.defenseimagery.mil; VIRIN: DN-SC-86-01099, Public Domain 10bm; By Kevin M. Gill - https://www.flickr.com/photos/53460575@N03/50513674188/, CC BY 2.0 16bl; By Magellan Team (NASA - Jet Propulsion Laboratory) - This image or video was catalogued by Jet Propulsion Laboratory of the United States National Aeronautics and Space Administration (NASA) under Photo ID: PIA00233., Public Domain 10-11bg; By NASA - [[:File:Venus,_Earth_size_comparison.jpghttps://astrogeology.usgs.gov/search/map/Venus/Magellan/Colorized/Venus_Magellan_C3-MDIR_Colorized_Global_Mosaic_4641mhttps://commons.wikimedia.org/wiki/File:The_Blue_Marble_(remastered).jpg]], Public Domain 15ml; By NASA/JPL-Caltech - https://www.jpl.nasa.gov/news/nasa-selects-investigations-for-future-key-planetary-mission; original archived at https://web.archive.org/web/20190202192152/https://www.jpl.nasa.gov/news/news.php?feature=4727 (image link), Public Domain 22-23bg. NASA: Images-assets.nasa.gov/image/GSFC_20171208_Archive_e001737/GSFC_20171208_Archive_e001737~orig.jpg 17bl; images-assets.nasa.gov/image/PIA18145/PIA18145~orig.jpg 11tr; images-assets.nasa.gov/image/s30-71-052/s30-71-052~orig.jpg 13br; images-assets.nasa.gov/image/PIA00254/PIA00254~orig.jpg 12-13bg.
Shutterstock: 19 STUDIO 20bl; Anna Marin N 20-21bg; Artsiom P 8-9bg; AstroStar 16-17bg; Buradaki 6br, 9tr; CSSF 360 11tr (background); FastMotion 18-19bg; Feng Cheng 14mr; Gidenilson 4-5bg; Janez Volmajer 24bg; NASA Images 1bg, 2-3bg; Steven_mol 6-7bg; Vovan 14-15bg.